THE AMERICAN POETRY SERIES

BOOKS BY SANDRA MCPHERSON

Patron Happiness (1983)

Sensing (1980)

The Year of Our Birth (1978)

Radiation (1973)

Elegies for the Hot Season (1970)

Patron Happiness

PATRON HAPPINESS

SANDRA McPHERSON

The Ecco Press

NEW YORK

Copyright © 1979, 1980, 1981, 1982
by Sandra McPherson
All rights reserved
First published by The Ecco Press in 1983
18 West 30th Street, New York, N.Y. 10001
Published simultaneously in Canada by
George J. McLeod, Limited, Toronto
Printed in the United States of America
The Ecco Press logo by Ahmed Yacoubi
Designed by Loretta Li
First Edition

Library of Congress Cataloging in Publication Data

McPherson, Sandra
  Patron happiness.
  (American poetry series, v. 24)
  I. Title.   II. Series.
PS3563.A326P3   1983   811'.54   82-11490
ISBN 0-88001-021-5
ISBN 0-88001-022-3 (pbk.)

Publication of this book was made
possible in part by a grant from
The National Endowment for the Arts.

ACKNOWLEDGMENTS

American Poetry Review: Alleys; The Delicacy;
   Discoveries, Mid-Letter; For Elizabeth Bishop;
   Ode to a Friend from the Early Sixties.
Antaeus: The Firefly; If the Cardinals Were Like Us;
   Man in an Old Myth; Pornography, Nebraska; 7, 22, 66;
   The Steps; Unitarian Easter; Earthstars, Birthparents' House;
   Ode Near the Aspen Music School.
Concerning Poetry: The Wheel.
crazyhorse: A Poem for My Teacher.
Field: Games; The Museum of the Second Creation;
   Two Poems on Definitions of *Bitch.*
Helix (Australia): Lifesaving.
The Iowa Review: The Anointing; Helen Todd: My
   Birthname; The Spa of the Posthumous.
The New Leader: Last Week of Winter.
The Paris Review: Night Vision.
Poetry: Black Soap; Diary—May 15, 1980—Twin Cities;
   The Jet Engine; Living Glass; Only Once;
   Preparing the Will, Three Generations; Urban Ode;
   Wings and Seeds; Writing to a Prisoner.
The Reaper: Last Week of Winter (revised form).
Watertable: Unexplained Absences.

Some of the poems have been revised since their first publication.

The second section of "Black Soap" is based on a passage in Colette's *Earthly Paradise.*

I am grateful for the support of the National Endowment for the Arts in the form of a writing grant for the year 1980. And I'm indebted to Leigh McLellan, who hand-printed some of these poems in *Sensing* (Meadow Press, 1980, San Francisco).

for Ellayn,
my sister,

and Bill,
my brother

Contents

III

Overheard today in the Lowie at the Hopi arts demonstrations . . .

BYSTANDER: *"Which part of potting do you like the best?"*

HELEN NAHA, "FEATHERWOMAN": *"Well, there are three dirty parts and two clean parts. The dirty part is molding, sanding, and slipping. The clean part is painting and firing. I guess I like them all."*

—my diary, March 7, 1981

The Firefly

Few master a form to be conspicuous in the night.
Sometimes I think I am the night,
Having nothing, not even a broken line.
The winter night across the neighborhood

Of past fireflies. Having lost even their slow
Radiance, their disconnections of someone
Pacing back and forth before a lamp,
Their teasing flight like the doubt in two voices:

Can I see you? and *Do you really see me?*
Day might see one,
Stopped, eating from the yellow ray-end
Of a dillblossom. But night after night

I am the stretch it once bit into
With hard catchable light,
Going in some direction, I never knew which
Until I saw it twice.

Games

I play pool. I aim toward the faces
   Across the room. My daughter
Takes these quarters for the pinball
   She plays with a dying

Butterfly on her left hand. It
   Will not leave, it is tired,
And all its strength is in its legs.
   I set it on my arm

Then give it back. I'll take her hand
   That way when dying, stick
Out my tongue, like its curled black one,
   Green crutch of a Kentucky

Wonder Bean, and *Look*, she cries,
   Its body fell away.
It's all wings and head. Short life
   Has culled mistaken

Parts and dropped the mite-sized heart and
   Killed the steering place.
Or else she did this, quickened its
   Death among the games

And flunked it too soon. And even so
   The golden-mica'd wings
Are best. She forgets it easily,
   Who never speaks of losing.

The Steps

MOTHER ONCE IN THE '40'S

He tells of the time she came swaying up the walk,
said she was going to pass out,
and would he assist her to the summer chair
where she could lie like a dentist's patient
trying to look like a bed of wind poppies.
He asked,

   Where were you?
     Where the leaves burrow:
     a store of webs,
     seeds and hair,
     some ash, in a place
     the light sucks every day.
     Dirt, fine as royalty,
     slivers with star points
     prying into submerged orbits.
     Where the stems go
     minus roots or leaves,
     and the maple seed dries,
     the rain misses.

   What were you doing?
     My feet held still
     and pulsed in the sun.
     The steps seemed the end,
     not a way up or down.
     I took off my shoes,
     pressed up a little paint,
     some slivers
     pulled out of the grain,
     the waves of the steps
     went on breaking.

What could you have been thinking of?
    Just servings
    of denser things,
    the method
    fly legs finally travel here,
    the work
    in piles of sawdust,
    and most everything falling
    through the angle opened
    by shrinking boards.
    There was no acreage
    to the place. It was more like
    a farm on a ladder.

And every other year since, he says,
when for some reason she faints,
he thinks it's because she once fell in with
light things, wanted to link with air the way they do,
and ultimately to be caught like part of a blossom
saved where it is laced
into a web.

Preparing the Will, Three Generations

She fills each little link
  Of the gold chains
We are asked to choose among
  With her tears;
She fears inheritance,
  The turning to shadow
Of fingers filling the opal rings
  We could select.

Oh don't be afraid,
  I say, Heaven
Is even more made of these things;
  That's where your
Grandparents are going; heaven
  Is even more
Lapis lazuli like these
  Piercing anemones
For Grandmother's ears.

Then those tears, too, appraised:
  She thinks she is
Too sinful and cannot
  Join them there.
Best ask for the ladderback chair,
  Or that glass sparrow
God's eye would glance
  Clear through:

Nothing directly changing hands,
    No sapphire watch,
Blue as the vein
    Under my mother's
Cirrus-thin wrist,
    For a hellion. Best ask
For the iron and board—
    And maybe the loudest radio—
Like they have in hell.

Two Poems on Definitions of Bitch

1

Don't curse the kite, I said, and on the third day
The red, nay-saying, unnimble kite
Flew much better and two swallows fought in her air.
The pinwheel did as well as in Alaska.
You lay on your back
As you do when I want you.
I watched a June bug piece together flight.
The kite had been stubborn in nothing.
Phoebe re-read her maroon diary, the one from her
                                        eleventh year.
Already it reminded her of things past,
While the kite logged hours in the air . . .

2

I ruffled the broad back of the red bitch
And unwrapped the turkey heart from my sack.
Her owners kept their eyebrows still.
This was the reward of friendship.
She ran on the sand, having fed on the heart of a bird.
She went and stood in the water, looking straight at the
                                        oncoming wave.
She danced away under the red kite.
I liked to lose her in the distance for it was no great loss.
What did the purple starfish think of her feet?
What did the orange starfish think of her feet
That were not there the next day
Or the next. The green anemones folded their fingers
Together as if they had just eaten the word *bitch*.
Those who are owned—take them a bite
In some old foil you've saved
And will save, battered as if by the heart.

Black Soap

1

White lather on black soap—
Maria's gift. It reminds me
Of when a woman died
And they handed me her ring.

Then they left to divide the roots for her.
Daylight went down there shining.
By accident, cleaning the hearth
Of a house to leave it for good,
I learned how to see
A star come out: work
My hand into the ashes.

2

"You've thrown a chestnut hull into the fireplace again,"
Said Colette's mother, "My clean ashes!"
Naughty Colette had soiled the washing ashes
Of applewood, poplar, and elm.
Stretched over the big cauldron
In the washhouse, hemp cloth held the ashes
The washwoman poured a jug of boiling water on.
They smelled almost sweet as the lye
Filtered into the mass of linen.
The air darkened with blue clouds.
In the smoking lava layer of ashes,
A few cinders of chestnut hulls,
The tannin's yellow stain.

3

Look for something
You've been every day of your life.
You said it was "lonely."
I'm certain it is also "clean."
My body's big years diminish soap.
My grandmother, whose diamond it was,
Had a stone in her tub.
I rubbed it on my feet
As later I walked,
Building little hoofs,
All summer shoeless on creek gravel.

That black bar of stone
In the widow's clean house,
That volcanic pumice skips
Over most hard places
But softens at least one.

4

Once there was a downpour of rain
They took as a judgment.
It confused her billowing, steaming skirts.
Another time—those times were hard—
The executioner let go the twisted hemp
From her neck sooner than he should
Because the flames reached his hands.
Nor would I, if I'd had to live then,
Put my hands into the fire

Those three hours it took to reduce her.
But after, I'd scrub all over
With the ashes of the still warm
Black heart of the witch.

Man in an Old Myth

NIGHT

The myth isn't sure how well he cares for himself.
He returns, charming the night
With a musical smoke,

And allays the locked heart of the little keyhole
After a clinking serenade.
Nominating all the wrong keys.

Oh the landlady, she won't mind,
She's left him a doughnut
So the phonograph won't play.

His list of passwords to his responsibilities
Is fuzzy—check the mousetrap and name
The mouse, lay to rest

The drooping alleyflowers . . . but let them stay
The night.
Tomorrow he'll gleam in the tub like fountains' pay.

MORNING

The sunlight enters him like an unbuttoned
Épée. A high piping from the tap
And the washcloth goes in.

Waxwings
Flip masked heads
And gold tails in the eaves.

Aspirin like a plectrum
Strums the lyre of his famous vocal cords.
His tongue is green but as a willow leaf.

He has affected a love of death; now he mirrors it.
Thinks it's a fine apology
When he both shaves and sings.

So he lives among his towels.
They are what morning means for him.
When morning leaves, he goes in search of her.

Alleys

For the man I'd marry I picked a white flower
Out of the dust behind a shed. The alleys
Are bare with such gifts—I'll pick up a penny

Or spots will be a dog approaching. It is
Not even a withered flower anymore,
But the dust of the first kind thing I did for him.

Later I brought in bouquets with creatures on them.
Voiceless, with increasing legs—not
The jays and doves I heard in alleys . . .

How long ago I was morning sick
In that city alley! Frightened
And leaning like a wino against the brick.

Trucks went there, and trash, and there
Was no delivered bird's egg in my path.
Now I am morning glad, all

Is pregnant outside me. I face the rabbit's
Victorious ears, the bumblebee, and mushrooms
On a fallen limb. There's not a house

Whose exit they don't call to,
Whose cries they don't keep
From heading into the street. These widths of sun . . .

A wren fusses inside a hedge; bones have been thrown
To the back of a fence. The dust
Is not all of kindness. I leave a bit

Of blue plate, do not steal the horseshoe
That perhaps I should. Who knows
Where anything is in a cycle? Alleys are behind us,

But sunflowers fall forward into them—
As if to call for rain in the ruts. While in our house
There is the opposite. His unfinished glass of water

Appears to beg me for a flower.

If the Cardinals Were Like Us

A FRIEND'S VOICE

Before I'm awake, the dreamlike
Courtesy could happen in fact—

The male places the sunflower seed
In his mate's bill.

I've seen it other mornings.
He'd seed a blush-red cloth, ruined

On a twig, if it were all
He had, my husband told me once . . .

When he does not come home,
I hope to wake to a plush bird,

A chant of flattery. I like it because
We do not have the vocabulary,

My daughter and I, to discuss
What's happened: the new day's

So bright you cannot see the porchlight on.

To come back to us, he rises
And his lover's cat

Claws up the bedstead to her side.
I find my bedtime book unmoved

From the sheet's smooth half,
And on my half the blood that—

As I've slept—has made this sheet as red
As it needs to be and ruined enough.

Now he's in our door
And telling us, "Breakfast,

Eclairs from the bakery for breakfast.
Come down."

7, 22, 66

Which doesn't belong in this group of three?—
Soap, Bible, stationery.
Two deal with creation;
So obviously the soap

Doesn't blend—
It can't wash away the fate
Of three of us trying to belong
To one another.

But on our honeymoon, from the key's first turn,
I thought the misfit was the Bible.
I was already with child
Beside the Gideon cover with its torch.

Fresh out of the shower, you judged each queen
For softness; I packed the stationery.
Even while we lay still,
Fog closed the window.

From the Port Townsend double on heavy pilings,
Tides growing barnacles and starfish
Under the bed, we did not take God's word
For a souvenir.

Rustling an atlas, catching the morning ferry,
You went on with me, into a life that had stolen you,
Asking that night for a decent room for two,
And puzzling out the number on its key.

Pornography, Nebraska

Once, on that highway where a traveler works hard
To remember what he loves intensely in this life,
   Because it is so endlessly bare,
   The highway I mean,   ⌐

I heard on our CB one trucker tell another
About tattoos around the areolas. About the hurt.
   The second man's
   Hadn't been as bad, but needling him elsewhere—

To recall a barberpole—
Caused definitive pain. Drunk when he started,
   He couldn't renege until the last prick of ink.
   It was sobering.

On this long journey out of cultivation, sage
At last outspices hay. Bulls twist up dust
   In an hourglass-shaped battle,
   Heads at the center.

A vulture on a fencepost
Like a single staked rose by a farmhouse . . .
   And still the voice of public confession
   Goes through the dotty illustrations on his body,

Forty-some, he says, like milemarkers to the border.
Then I remember losing him,
   If only on the radio.
   It was at last so dark I felt the way I did

When once I was actually leaving someone I dearly loved.
Moonlight traveled
   The bedspring spiral of my notebook
   In which I recorded the distance

From him by the fuel burned.
Wherever the pictured man was, somewhere a spanker
   Like "PJ's" back in Muscatine
   Performed astonished love

As a way of testing out his story, seeing
If she could believe him.
   New voices
   Took over the channel

But they only tattled on a patrol,
Who soon appeared, his outwitted chase-light off.
   Then one last voice—
   A siren at the stateline,

Crying higher, calling out.
It involved catching no one. Lightning
   Had fired the ranges. All the Pine Bluffs,
   Wyoming, Fire Department volunteers

Stopped dreaming. They knew they must cool
Their nakedness; the wail said they must drive,
   As fast as they could,
   Away from their beds.

The Delicacy

Friend, remember how you showed us beasts love beauty?
We were wading in your lake with bluegills and you said,
Be careful, you will lose your beauty marks

To their little jaws. We were a delicacy. From us they
                                            purchased
The darkest part of the skin, only what contrasts on us.
And it was more than a pinch or sting,

It's a sensation of hunger
That makes us spring off the bottom and swim out deep
And safe. "No blue stripes on cheeks; no red on fins;

Old individual's belly coppery red or brassy."
As others see you, I think these indicate,
Who would have you all one shade then wouldn't have you.

At your full table later, over muskellunge and lemon,
We read in the book the fish that liked us
Has certain maxillaries "wholly wanting." Your gourmet
                                            bluegill:

It lives in the eye of the beholder, it swims the vitreous
Humor, would eat even your blind spot!
But we think we can paddle out there until all

Goes dark, and we are wholly desirable, and too much.

for M.H.

Writing to a Prisoner

Wet shells in my wool pockets,
A feeling of walking as if on America
Among stones of different homelands,
The speckled, the veined, the spotted,
Agate and opaque gray-green regimes,
The rusty drip of a slow iron spring,
The stranding of oysters' empty compartments,
Ruffled chassis still hinged,
Castle among shells;
This morning the blue inlet shines in fog
Unbroken by horizon,
Only the noiseless dives of black and
                         white buffleheads,
No splash as they surface,
The limp long neck of a dead grebe,
Each khaki foot like a spray of buckeye leaves,
Its skewery beak, clamped on a kelp strand,
Pointing toward one boat going out;
The bird has no eye
And a gull, probably, has pecked right through the
                                          breastbone
To the heart;
When I am here, I understand even my own markings,
Those small things among all dwarfed human things.

Somewhere in this wild neighborhood your prison
Locks its fifteen hundred men
Away from curiosity.
If only you could laugh at the ridiculous head-shaking
Of the sea worm
Or wonder that the heron chooses to be lonely,
A still tide-measurer.

Of course I am afraid to correspond with you,
To ask an honest question,
Even to praise my daughter,
Or display the outsider's perpetual acquitting craziness
                                        of passion.
I think of the deer close beyond your wall,
How they roam beneath safe gunbarrels in the towers.
What if only I am writing you?
Then it's too much responsibility
To write you the great beauty
The moonless tide book is dried from;
To translate the wit of puffins
Diving deep as octopi for trollers' bait;
And demonstrate how common
I am in the droves from which you've picked one name.

Returned to this opening sea-land
All my wrong-headed tension bolts right and free,
All clumsiness and backache and obsession,
Just by standing a moment on a changing shore,
Widening and narrowing,
Beside a chiton cast up
And a stone shanghaied out for a voyage
In exchange.

Living Glass

The pine-sheltered benches, the cliff path
Lined with fencegates and pink wild rose
Took me then toward the small salt-windowed seaside
                                            school,
And now, in my longing to escape from those I hurt,

Rebuild before my eyes to throw a sea-light
On the bare, inland, sleeping feet of those I love.
Suddenly the goat kid in its driftwood pen bleats for them,
Their faces simplified while I watch them wake.

Their clothes, swirled on the floor,
Remind me of the lengthy row the tide makes
Of opal and living glass, miles of jellyfish
Retiring, some navy blue as bottle-stones.

Their deaths increase their hue.
The clear ones lay a glass stairway
Bannistered by seamarks, and often this is the path
I walk beside to the distant schoolbell,

Imagining a strand of kelp the bellrope
And each jellyfish a ghost
Who, living mornings, pulled.
Death has no depth like where they lived.

And so, as the great tide shies back
Around its water-breathing fleets, death
Is what they pull against,
The whole way to the bell.

There, with wind to spare,
Lame people with canes stroll miles
And their grandchildren stay put, dissolving castles,
Burying each other till it seems

They can't escape. Under their low eyes
Mica mirrors all its sources around the world
And the tide rolls in, brown and blue
As two sides of a swallow twisting in the air.

Somehow I've hurt you. Sit with me here
And watch the children burst the sandwalls and climb free.
Follow with me the sea's champagne glasses
To the schoolhouse, and

Taking turns we'll sit awakened
In the summer-empty seats, the other teaching
With chalk-covered hands. Then we'll wash ourselves
Of any bitter knowledge with the sands.

The Spa of the Posthumous

PEARL KARSTEN SPEAKS

They have prepared the mud. We try
    The rest cure, the thorn house, the inhalatorium.
The men tip their hats, women twirl
Their canes to each other on the walk.
    Green and sky, pink sun canopies . . .
We drink the pumped waters. The orchestra tromps.

I like the continuous balcony. Each room
    Has antlers (antelope and roe deer),
Pewter jug, pewter plate, pewter bottle.
I get the pewter bowl from over the wainscoting,
    Ladle bouillon from the tub in the hay-box.
I unfold the bed, draw the deep

Red Pullman curtains. When I sleep
    I am further along the family tree:
I can hardly remember the low German.
I hear lo of angels, low
    Chatter gulfs my pink casket.
But it's really not finished: the digger has

Not quite prepared my therapeutic mud.
    A shovel leans against a tree
Behind the family. Look at their caution!—
Wary of the rootless fly-green grass-cloth
    They step up on to worship,
Afraid it is hollow underneath . . .

I remember a brink like that: the day I watched them dig
  A man who was building our sewer
Out of the landslide.
They were looking for his black hand
  In the lithosphere, for the slope
Of his hard hat. Now they are looking

For us all, the ruddy bath attendants
  Digging us out. Help me, sir;
Give me your arm as I step to the duckboards,
Take the handshower to my old skin
  To separate the clay
From what I know as myself.

For Elizabeth Bishop

The child I left your class to have
Later had a habit of sleeping
With her arms around a globe
She'd unscrewed, dropped, and dented.
I always felt she *could* possess it,
The pink countries and the mauve
And the ocean which got to keep its blue.
Coming from the Southern Hemisphere to teach,
Which you had never had to do, you took
A bare-walled room, alone, its northern
Windowscapes as gray as walls.
To decorate, you'd only brought a black madonna.
I thought you must have skipped summer that year,
Southern winter, southern spring, then north
For winter over again. Still, it pleased you
To take credit for introducing us,
And later to bring our daughter a small flipbook
Of partners dancing, and a ring
With a secret whistle. —All are
Broken now like her globe, but she remembers
Them as I recall the black madonna
Facing you across the room so that
In a way you had the dark fertile life
You were always giving gifts to.
Your smaller admirer off to school,
I take the globe and roll it away: where
On it now is someone like you?

The Wheel

The platform vanishes. The wheel's miraculously
Balanced on snow. Its chairs lie packed
With the merry-go-round's beasts
For Charlie to take far south.

No footprints between the wheel and the ticket booth
But his, fresh. He inspects the spines,
Wires, gears. Frames in uncountable triangles
Still will make you dizzy.

Then suddenly the ragtime's playing
Over the yellow pig on the carousel. It's summer
Too for the saddled chicken,
Who has a rider. But no one chooses,

This time, the black horse. The bandannaed lady
Slides tickets through the windowspace
To her old man. His ribbed hands
Have spun generations. Children who rode,

Grown up now, now believe
The hitching post goes through the heart.
Again Charlie watches that pregnant girl:
Wait until fall, he thinks, leaves will pause

On her stomach before they slip.
Next year she'll be thin and bring her child
To me, this girl who moves like one of my
Animals, smoothly forward, burdened up and down.

Like the snow that will stay till it recedes
To a single spot on his old head, Charlie's rides
Stay open until the miniature train's last turn
Carries hickory leaves and only two of us:

A sad child whose cat, she says, has died;
And in the tailcar myself. Knowing many
Angels too, I'll ride to keep my feet
As silent off the ground as theirs.

for Robert Huff

A Poem for My Teacher

A hat shop where one's mother
Shifts a courageous shape
About her hair,

A seamstress's where
The gray coat has two secret pockets
Which snuff down your hands,

A stop for hangers at the laundress's
In time to see a train
Shake every window,

Then to the shut-in with her sheet
Concealing something
Like a sleeping pet,

That night I'll sit on the porch,
Just five or six,
And let myself go blind
Until the light comes on.

But though you lie in the shaking California ground
You know the beginnings
Once they endlessly start.

This is your student in each small town chair.
We don't know what you've lived for
And we've come to live.

We're half-formed, tongue-tied, mental-blocked.
One boy loves vowels—
In his seat he sways;

One girl
Has filled the air with cinnamon
In six words,
Five. The future

Tears the building down,
Scatters
Our drab garden's tans and olives, gray

And ivy black,
Those walls fall, what
If we are all condemned . . .

But though you lie in the shaking California ground
The tremor is familiar, loose it
And jot until the little light comes on.

for Roberta Holloway

Unexplained Absences

A pure white robin.
From Connecticut,
C.M. Jones
found it, 1887.
Its bill and feet

yellowed anyway
like a plastic cross.
The eye waived
color so the blood shows through.
Its visibility

rends woods. And voice? A
common *chk?* or some
white caustic
sheet music in the skies above
a bride raccoon

without a mask, all
in white down like thin
Bible paper.
Her nose is black just like the mel-
anistic mink,

or grackle with al-
bino tail. Animal
paper plates
usable only once. Two champagne
meadow mice,

1929.
A birchbark muskrat:
white inside?
No, insides stain, albinos
eat color: red

flies, blue mussels, green
apples. Our first white
hair turns for
albino wholeness, a welcome
blanking out,

the pure white red-tailed
hawk striking with more
than usual
warning. Conspicuous things
try to hunt;

if it were I, you'd
live because I was
so obvious.
Yet this predator is spotless
and died fat.

Disbelieving its approach
was the grassy
mouse's last delight.

Discoveries, Mid-Letter

—I can't translate much,
But I know the symbol for the sun:
Two empty boxes, or the dusty corners
Of a sunporch. Will they never
Tell the weather?
The Iharas left this delicate letter
Crushed behind a desk drawer,
Ballpoint Japanese
On paper thin enough to divide a soul.

Took J. to the place
Where you and I saw the rat.
This time was different—my first
Green heron flew under the low trees
And chose a branch
That strawed up winter life
From that blank pure springwater.
Is it gloom if it startles and shifts?
Lovelier yet,
The bird was immature,
Streaked, and unknowledgeably late for this meridian.

Phoebe keeps cutting larger and larger scarlet letters,
Wants to know exact material and style.
Yes, she can translate the A,
Ornate or plain. She stalks me
And suddenly I'll feel something held against my back.
She tries it there, before I'll admit
To wearing it face on.
I like it, I say,
I like anything you make for me.

Frail characters!
And they will keep appearing, surreptitious surprises.
We must be unready for them.

Only Once

Thrifty with light, the five-and-dime
Plays a remnant into the hands
Of the young widow: she is making
Her first apron, to work in the kitchen
Of someone who races greyhounds,
Sleek as dimes.
But nickels are the bulldogs of money,
And the young woman, my only aunt,
Soon breeds an ugly litter
To sell for pin-money and debts.
Sex as a possibility
Of prosperity was something our family
Thought of only once.

Like our one-time purchase of string
In that squeaky-floored dimestore,
Aunt's enterprise becomes unique:
It is curtailed by thrift.
We untie cord on packages, string
From balloons, find kite-tangles.
The short length, the ephemeral, we combine.
Any string's recognizable
As binding though it does little
But curl, grayly essential, in a drawer—
A frail leash.

And the apron?—worth at least
A dog's seeing, brightened with leftover
Loops of chartreuse embroidery thread.
She winds her hands in it and leads me
Into the yard-kennel where, not much weaned
Myself, I see the nurse of ugliness

In the beauty of her motherhood.
In the milk-rinsed sunlight,
I don't feel poor.
I watch my aunt's fortune grow,
The puppies do well—
They wrangle and eat,
They do not sell.

Night Vision

A FRAGMENT FOR LUCRETIUS AND OTHERS

Heaven bribes me;
But for a dream
I have only to lie down.
I am the judge
And sleep shameless and just
Among perfect examples,
Scripts, idols, panoramas, mazes.
 A speech-cure,
Sleep warrens laughter
And bulges a snore. "When I allowed myself
Images and pompous expressions,
A god warned me in my sleep,
Censured my writings,
Brought me back to a natural style."
Perhaps, but didn't his eyes strain and leap?
Could he read, his hand
On skids, trying to write with the eyes
Shut? Even Helen Keller
Couldn't feel the pages
She felt lovingly
In the great book dreamt on her knee.
 Night is
Black mail. Blackout
Within blackout, then suddenly
Cerulean lapstrakes, raspberry-
Colored houses; the heaven below,
Snobbish if wistful,
Jealous of being remembered,
Wounded when I leave it each morning.
 Years of berceuses

Hummed for love of the nightmare,
Frisky, arcadian, ponytailed.
It has us bedridden.
The old dream of being lost in insulation
Turns inability to find you
Or a place to make love.
The hug, the pit of the stomach, salivation—
I convince the horse
There are pleasures in being human.
Young, I was crushed by a giant;
Now each attentive nonesuch
Looks where he is going.
   Serious wishes: to own
Or be enthralled; be fugitive,
Sought, to hide
In majesty; be guilt-pleased,
Act selfish, receptive, intense.
For buildings to need maps;
For scenery to be magnetic,
Light steep; for graves'
Cumulonimbi to circulate;
For shoes to be round-toed
And money extinct.
   For we'd rather not bargain
For pre-owned dreams, wizened hands,
Odds, lumber, cat scratches, weeds,
Less than would fill a pipe,
Worshipful blending though they make
Of all we have known and desired.
Start afresh, fatigued.
If it's true
I dream some work I did today,

Then that work must be beautiful,
All day's dismay
Laboratory of the chemist
Overcome by inventing
The first ether.

The Jet Engine

A little bit of the body at morning is
   Poison; a lot
Of the mind is ether. Lying there
   Level between them
Is difficult, anxious as fuel
   In a dory tank on the ocean.

Inviting as the blue water looked
   Out the guest-bed window
On a day of enfolding visibility,
   I questioned my hostess
About the dawn ghosts that filled the room
   And me. Never,

She said, was she afraid in day.
   But she could tell me
In her automated kitchen what
   Shook her once:
The stovepipe fan big as a ship's funnel
   Sucked up all the gas

And threw a fireball to the autumn woods.
   Was it fire
Or fumes that scared her most? Now
   The pokey electric range
Takes us in a teacup slowly into morning,
   Pilotless.

But, friend, I've turned myself quickly
    Out of bed ever since.
For leaving your place I saw a huge and tangled
    Shiny thing hauled
Gingerly down the Interstate. It was not
    Yet self-lifting. Heart

Of an enormous plane, it took its own
    Company exit.
Not like its sistership
    Whose finished body disappeared
Above the long paved field, beyond
    The speed of the voice

Where it's calm, this still bumped
    Chattering along.
It was just going through that time
    In its life when a jet engine
Rides the bed of a truck—
    Closer to the ground

Than it must ever be again for people.

for Gwen Head

III

Earthstars, Birthparents' House

Geasters. She bent down
At the dappled base of the tree,
And among the brown leaves
Geasters stood up.

Oranges peel like these,
She said. Rinds bent back.
When it rains, their legs swell up
And walk.

> Stranger feet
> Than mine
> All these years
> Outside your door.

Wings and Seeds

Hiking a levee through the salt marsh,
My birthmother and I. She is not teaching
Me to read and write but to believe
The hummingbird mistrusts its feet,
Weak below its feisty wings.

We trample brass buttons and chamomile,
As if to concern ourselves no more
With clothing and tea.
We twine hands, we trade heavy binoculars.
The clouds are coming from far out on the sea
Where they'd only the fetch to ruffle.

Separately our lives have passed from earthy passion
To wilder highliving creatures with wings.
With our early expectancies
Did we come to think ourselves a flight of nature?

Terns flash here, four dolled-up stilts in a pool,
Dozens of godwits a thick golden hem on the bay—
You'd think we too knew how to find
Our way back to this home ground.

I was a child of pleasure.
The strong pleasurable seeds of life
Found each other.
And I was created by passion's impatience
For the long wait till our meeting.

Helen Todd: My Birthname

They did not come to claim you back,
To make me Helen again. Mother
Watched the dry, hot streets in case they came.
This is how she found a tortoise
Crossing between cars and saved it.
It's how she knew roof-rats raised families
In the palmtree heads. But they didn't come—
It's almost forty years.

I went to them. And now I know
Our name, quiet one. I believe you
Would have stayed in trigonometry and taken up
The harp. Math soothed you; music
Made you bold; and science, completely
Understanding. Wouldn't you have collected,
Curated, in your adolescence, Mother Lode
Pyrites out of pity for their semblance
To gold? And three-leaf clovers to search
For some shy differences between them?

Knowing you myself at last—it seems you'd cut
Death in half and double everlasting life,
Quiet person named as a formality
At birth. I was not born. Only you were.

The Anointing

Benedict makes us look bad—
All greased muscle, like a porpoise.
Like the bowl of olives, Benedict
Is oiled holy, green and slippery
In his godfather's arms. He is
Already the man they want,
Handsome and nude, such a man
As desire accepts and accepts.

A lamb has been sacrificed.
Black with coal, white with garlic,
It is seared on flat swords. This too
We accept, we longingly accept.
Green grapes mound high, like fingertips
Of the priest upon the child's body
When the boy's eyes are so
Black, rebellious as they cry
In terror of the chant, the soul-deep water.

All the guests know what it is
To dedicate a life. It's what
May sadden our pianos, or wedge a stop
Beneath words. But in the fresh air
Under the smoke of the offering,
The new man crawls toward us—
Not young, not immature.
Sculptured idol of the eternal,
The holy child crawls across the grass
To kiss our feet.

for Benedict Kegham Goekjian

Lifesaving

You and I are like an old married couple
Since I pulled you from the swimming pool
(The "blueberry pie" you once described it)

In the evening sunshine of Dunsmuir, California.
My parents, that old married couple, stretched just
                                        beyond seeing
On the motel lawn chairs. They were wearing
Fresh clothes and smelled of shower soap.

They watched the rotating colored light play
Through the fountain and over the petunias
(Which must have thought it weird,

In their simple mind). The dust was settling
Out of the air from the highway project.
We had been going south all day and tomorrow
We would go south.

And they never found out. Your father
Never found out. Only in my mind
Do I hear your close call.

We dried off, it was a perfect evening,
The motel owner was playing "The Blue Danube" on his
                                        piano.
Mt. Shasta changed in the sunset like the petunias.
You looked over at some teenagers kissing in a shadow;

And you said, "So that's what love is."

for Phoebe

Last Week of Winter

Horrible tinctures of ginger and cayenne and sage for
colds,
From the *Back to Eden* book that recommends

Blue violet, white pine, rock rose which we do not have,
Have given way to turned earth smells and hourly
checkups

For breakthroughs from seeds, cavernous or should I say
cadaverous
Peas, and Burpee's new golden beet that does not bleed.

My friend has set a fine lunch for us of lox,
Croissants, alfalfa tea with a leaf of mint. Her body

Takes a new turn weekly we must discuss: "We are not
New minted any more." Sometimes it is a four-

Mile run or mood or dry eyes, insomnia, or piano pain.
Or achievement of her narrow fingers into Chopin's hair-

Fine, hair-thick notes. I love to see her razzled, flickery,
Turbid like the winter floods. Dismissive, she shows

Old bundled photos of the snow. She wants her picture
Taken well before she gets too old.

I say, Get old, use black and white, it's more
Revealing, you want to be more shocking, old . . .

But why should she tell me then
She is a secret mother? These years I've known her!

She gave away a child instinctively
So her own life could begin.

Yes, I lean toward her, *My birthmother too,* seeing my blanket
Become her blindfold, went on to her giftedness,

Gave me away, took on term after term of physics,
Homework not housework, her knowledge was born

Despite motherhood threatening to push
Her body further from the desk.

I rejoice in this: that her arms reaching to gather the
                                    numbers like plums
Also embraced me reaching for words, you reaching for
                                    octaves, your daughter

For some talent entirely her own. . . .

And I whisper across the picnic cloth, in the strong
Burning smell of narcissus: *"Flowering plum,*

Buson said, *and the dancing ladies go to buy obis."*

Diary May 15, 1980 - Twin Cities

The cook invited us into the alley.
It was just dawn. But the dawn
  Of the cafe's anniversary
  And the champagne began.

Never mind we'd never eaten there at all,
Nor that the famous Al's Breakfast
  Is minuscule—a wall,
  One row of stools,

Another row of waiting customers,
A wall. It's beloved.
  Three glasses each,
  We watched the cork fly

Like a hummingbird across the roof. . . . At ten
C. started the Bug from underneath,
  Its dandelion yellow transformed
  To a seed-burst

Where he cracked the windshield with his fist
(Not long ago, he admits,
  In terms of human evolution).
  The seats radiate stuffing

Like beaten, sun-cooked dolls.
The license plate suggests no American word
  And stammers us
  To a place where we learn

To spell our names in hieroglyphs—
A symbol for a sound; an ankh, a bird—
    In front of a mummy.
    He looks sweaty

Like a roast, but holier. So this
Is a throat that sang,
    That called in cows,
    That a woman

Kissed deep into on a riverbank. . . .
The vista we drive out to
    Looks as far away
    As the mummy had looked back in time:

The bluff we climb
Isn't frightening to look down from;
    It sees a harp of routes—
    Rails, river, runway, road—

Spreading and shining from downtown.
Before a baby Mississippi,
    Double engines pull house-size
    Boxcars like a marigold tugging

At bricks. Shoulderbladed planes
Waft over barges' cargoes
    From this distance
    Stable and glideable;

We make like we could push them with a finger.
It's Third Grade social studies;
   The next unit
   Will be communications,

A fan of wires shining like a grackle's tailfeathers
And bothered only in unison
   By the wind.
   That blue air blows through

The woof of worn bluejeans.
If there can be such a thing as tight
   Open places,
   Here they are, like guitar

Strings. The warp has been the first
To go, to use a phrase
   The widows of my family like. . . . River,
   When I have navigated,

I've steered by a chart's half-words:
SFT and YL that water shrank
   From SoFT, YeLlow, RocK;
   GRaSs, Mud, BlUe.

The bottom approaches and flees,
The fathometer can sight-read.
   But I suppose those little Lears
   That land smooth

As anaesthesia and take off like champagne
Have no abbreviations to describe
   The heights, don't say
   The air smells GRaSsy here,

Or, in this flyway are how many
Of the hundred different birds
   In the pharaohs' alphabet?
   C. had to start the car

With a flashlight, the way the sun
Jars this valley alive at dawn
   So that traffic inspires the air
   To follow in and out—

Harmonica dynamics. C. pinched a tiny
Hohner from his pen pocket.
   Even it
   Was small because of the distance—

Replica of that one Schirra
Took to the moon,
   Which was new
   Yesterday.

The Museum of the Second Creation

The dioramacist does not know
How the Creator shows emotion.
So he flings the passenger pigeon across the sunset
As a guess. And the pigeons look joyous.
In fact, he says, I could call it a sunrise,
No one will ever know.

If there is a whole
Table of feet, and one
Of skulls, and a rugful of antlers, a bench of pelts,
A skinner has loved to give samples to touch,
A collector has strewn away the danger
By pooling big and little teeth.

And the taxidermist must be happy each time
He's given a weasel to stuff, maybe that's
His favorite animal, and best if it's a Least
Weasel, once full of night courage, at the neck
Of a cat or the heel
Of a cow.

Who fills museums
Loves to recreate little horses.
I have seen them in most big cities, little horses
In a rodeo through swamps, little horses
That could companion us
Like dogs.

Joining the fruit-bat's bones,
The stringer loves to reveal its outgrown fingers,
Strokes of fossil longer than our own. Flying on a wire
At dusk, its mouseflesh gone, its tarp wings rotted,
Big starlight hands.
The visitor says: Lost love, your body is so

Recreated in me
That I can look in the glass
Polished round the animal we loved the most
And see how nearly real you are.
What reincarnation is there? What can I learn
From the egg-gatherer

Sitting on his license to clean a new lilac shell,
Turning its most ecstatic face upward?
What can I glean from the late-late janitor
Sweeping up moths that fall
Through seal ribs strung near the light?
Their wings are now his—

Their sparkle's on his broomstraws.

Unitarian Easter

Entering here, I hope the confetti
Can jazz up a burden.

The pastor, for instance, calling birds, head back,
Or dancing an old French dance, hopping and kicking.

And now the congregation winds around the chancel,
Carrying damp, strapping forsythia sprigs, slanting them
into a vase
Beside the kotoist, her song plucked and bent, a few
blossoms raining on the strings.

God's weather today—sandals in puddles.
The moment of silence—raindrops on the roof, no
comment
On the matter of God.

Ode to a Friend from the Early Sixties

The pre-Divinity majors I once knew
Have all become gods by now.
Their wives were always goddesses.
But you and I were trained by weeds and boulders,
Graduating to a part of nature.

It was a lovely mountain: no winter
But staggered buds set for any month,
Always a few blossoms rushing things,
One of us always asking,
Who is the father?

In those days I write, "It is terrible
To go into the Commons: the odor
Of food is the stink of destruction.
The choice to sit alone
Or with cliques over breakfast

"Is even anguish. I can't talk
In the morning; I stumble conversing
At any hour. I also eat too much!"
We both inherit a lot
Of Conservatism, try to fly

On one wing, the right. But in two
Years' time it's all been taxed away.
Poor and radical, we reject our shoes
As muffling the truth.
We vote

And put these decades on. Those backrests,
The boulders, took twenty years off.
But still the olives fall on walks
Dappled like appaloosa rumps,
Culverts fill

With calla lilies, dry hillsides birthing
Wildflowers just taller than a toe.
And again we cry that the demons
Don't even make the papers; that we know
Dictatorial

Political murders speak clearly
To those who can't read. Where
Is the Divine? Twenty years more everlasting?
I don't know. Sometimes we go on celebrating
The fake birth of the eternal.

for M.S., November 1981

Ode Near the Aspen Music School

Two or three colors, two or three sounds govern
us more, determine our fate more than the
endless babbling of everyday give and take.

—GEORGE SEFERIS

Those melodies from the weeds—
A kid is making a xylophone
Out of broken glass.
She has perfect pitch.
She plays under a low purple light
From a storm coming on,
The thunder
Back of her song.

Girl, do you believe in black rainbows?
I saw them at my few symphonies,
As a child in the balcony,
Black bands of classic musicians,
Bent over the stage as around a cello,
The rays of the harpstrings showing through.
The chosen wore dignity; a player had to be a virtuoso
To win a part in the light
Of a black rainbow.

Oh, I've seen storms side to side
Cross the Mississippi
With light like raw wood
(Where we get our word *beam*)
To part them,
To fascinate a woman standing in the movement
Of the head cloud's shadow,
With her rake and apron.
With her back to a rainbow.
Wait till she sees it! I thought.

But in Aspen,
In the dust about to melt in the storm
Like chocolate, darken like dry cocoa
In a filling cup,
White-bloused musicians
Pass our door towards the tent,
Each one alone and early,
Thinking of the great scale
They soon will be part of.

The only perfect pitch I have
Is seeing numbers in color.
Even counting seconds after the lightning
I cannot escape a blue four
Or a yellow two.
A hummingbird rushes my beat:
He hangs pointing at my irises
As a smiling sprout will hold up an object,
Old key, even dangerous glass,
Too close to one's eyes.
Studious, the hoverer hums a few bars, they are green,

And suddenly the sirens wind up,
Wild and down, wild and down, five times.
The liquor is blowing in my heavy glass.
Smoke roils up from the yellow hillside
Opposed to the storm.
No red, peach, green, no indigo and more;
Yet these two boiling half-arches—
The storm and the smoke—
When they meet are not our black rainbow.

Ours is accumulating
From the solos
We heard on our walks,
Suddenly, from casements and interiors,
From a piccolo behind a hedge.
Solos now silent inside those formal musicians
Passing us, converging,
Mopping the dust off their shoes.

Now, hands resting in their basic dark laps,
They must be two
Or three beats away,
The rain just a mile,
The wind beginning to fill
A lapse of yesterday's violinist:
A sun-whitened shirt
Left out on the line.

Fate does not manage the colors and sounds;
What will become of us
In no way masters
The naive little theme
That makes our weedy percussions count.
Our governor is that one of the spectrum in black
Who raises a triangle,
Preparing us to hear what we will love
For the first time.

Urban Ode

I almost caught the bentwood chair
Flung across the soup joint at me.
    But I was hungry.
    The boy with the flying anger

Was quietly dusted out. Who
Knows him? Knows if he's mean
    Or just unwanted? Loneliness
    Used to feed a lot of us.

Bread and cheese, dinner alone;
The company of large empty vessels
    In galleries; one hour with
    A shrink and fifty at a good

Concealed piano that I knew—
That's how my Insufficiency was spent.
    But have we spent up the whole void
    Now we've lost our loneliness,

Plain happy to sidestep elaborate Freud?
After that soup I saw a windowshopping woman
    Walk into a street merchant's shelves
    Of pots until they all

Came down, perfection
In bowling, and lay about her toes
    Like segments of a mud facial
    She laughed over, crying. The potter,

Speechless, sold her the whole
Destruction. Out of loneliness, I've been violent
   To empty containers—
   A baby bottle slung against the wall

Left only a nipple in shag, and safety
Glass. Phoebe was full. Infancy
   Needs no romance. A child
   Today was chasing around a bush

That was not empty—"Ava, Ava," she cried,
"Come see the jay!" But Ava
   Had seen one before, she said,
   The shrub was vacant for her,

She saw no joy in the blue life.
Still the dress flew round and round
   The little cedar, outside
   At first, then into it.

And the girl who made that möbius
Was never separate from the jay again,
   Never objective, never
   Maunderingly subjective, she

Who had seen many.
In all her running, she'd run out of loneliness.
   What do you think? Can such
   Riches fall into our lives?

What do you think, Patron Happiness?